# Speed Bumps

## Lindy Lynch's Journey into Cancer

Other Works by Kathy Wagenknecht

*Away to Me*

*Come Bye*

*That'll Do*

*The 33rd Bennie Town Crow*

*Leaving Independence*

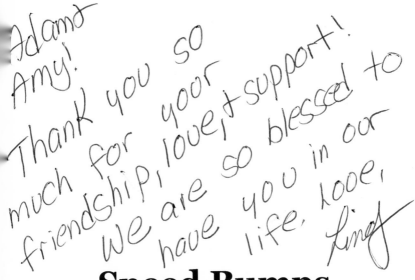

Adam &
Amy!
Thank you so
much for your
friendship, love, + support!
We are so blessed to
have you in our
life, Love,
Lindy

# Speed Bumps

## Lindy Lynch's Journey
## into Cancer

### Kathy Wagenknecht

White Wagon Books

Published by **White Wagon Books**

ISBN-13:  **9781730721137**

Copyright © **2018** by **Kathy Wagenknecht**
All rights reserved

Printed in the United States of America

# Dedication

For Lindy Lynch, one of the bravest people I know,
and for her Village –
the team she has assembled who support her in her journey

# Foreword

At the end of May, 2018, two of my friends came to me on the same day with the same request: would I meet with a local woman who wanted help writing a book, maybe ghost-write it for her.

I have been around long enough to know that multiple requests on the same day from unrelated sources probably should be given my attention. I said "Yes."

Two weeks later, I met Lindy Lynch for the first time. I knew who she was beforehand. Nobody could live in Bennington, Vermont, for long without at least hearing of her. She was leading or active in many civic organizations and their projects. I had a vague recollection that there had been a fundraiser for her because of a breast cancer diagnosis, and I knew she and her husband had owned a local bar and restaurant where I had eaten several times.

Lindy started telling me her story. She was funny, sincere, and inspiring as she described her journey through injury, her husband's cancer, and her own.

It didn't take me long after speaking with Lindy, and looking at her notebooks, to see that she was serious about wanting to create a book to share her story and what she had learned. And that she didn't know how to go about it.

I did know how to go about writing a book after having published five in the past few years, but I didn't know much about ghost writing.

Together we decided that an approach of two voices, mine as the narrator and Lindy's in direct quotations, would be the most honest approach since I did not know her well enough to try to be her ghost.

We met when Lindy was well enough to do so. I recorded her phone calls when she was not. Together we created the book that is intended to tell Lindy's story, pass on her accumulated knowledge, and help you get to know this extraordinary woman.

My hope is that you learn as much from Lindy as I have.

Kathy Wagenknecht
October, 2018

**Speed bumps** … are the common name for a family of **traffic calming** devices that use vertical deflection to slow motor-vehicle traffic in order to improve safety conditions.

Wikipedia contributors. "Speed bump." *Wikipedia, The Free Encyclopedia*. Wikipedia, The Free Encyclopedia, 19 Jul. 2018. Web. 29 Jul. 2018

Nobody's life is a freshly paved road forever. But the first fifty years of Lindy's were mostly smooth. There were potholes occasionally – drifting in college before becoming an Army nurse, two divorces, career changes, geographical relocations – that she had to navigate around, but by the time she and Kevin were married and running a successful restaurant together, Lindy Lynch was in her lane.

She was well-respected in Bennington, Vermont, where she was an active member of many of the town's boards and committees such as the Bennington County Child Care Association, North Bennington School Board, and the Chamber of Commerce, where she honed her skills as a leader and event planner.

Her children were grown and living their own lives, and her grandchildren were a source of delight.

It was during this active, productive time in her life, in the midst of planning for the annual Garlic Fest, that Lindy slammed into her first major speed bump.

A speed bump can serve to slow you down, to make you pay attention. But if you hit one at full speed, it can feel as if the bottom of your car fell off.

Or in Lindy's case, as if she dropped down a rabbit hole, where, like Alice, she found everything afterward had changed.

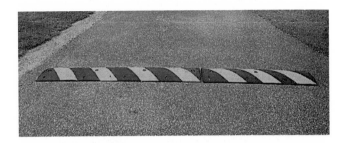

# First Bump

## The Rabbit Hole

It was August, 2010, in the middle of set-up for the annual Garlic Fest, an arts, crafts, culinary, and herbal festival featuring "the stinking rose," and Lindy had gone to the small building on the grounds that was serving as a deli to get a cup of coffee. She opened the door, stepped in, and there was no floor. The trap door to the cellar had been left open.

She dropped straight to the cellar floor, landing on her right shoulder and head. She lay on the floor, screaming in pain, realizing that her head and the entire right side of her body were damaged.

People arrived to help her. They called the rescue squad, and took her to the Southwestern Vermont Medical Center's (SVMC) Emergency Room in Bennington.

> There was a lot of craziness. I was screaming, "Garlic Fest, Garlic Fest! It's got to go on. Get my clipboard!"

It was chaos in the ER as they tried to diagnose what was wrong. After a CT scan, they determined that I needed immediate surgery. I had a concussion; I had a shoulder and humerus break. All the bones in my upper arm were broken. I had to go into immediate surgery. The whole shoulder had to be put together with a plate and 17 screws.

It was the right arm. I'm right-handed. Of course. I had a concussion, facial abrasions, everything on the right side of my body was damaged.

I made it through surgery. I was strapped down. I couldn't move at all. I spent several days in the hospital, went through hellacious pain, and then recovered at home.

I was terrified of stairs. My raised-ranch house has two short sets of stairs, so I just stayed downstairs.

I stayed there for a long time with round-the-clock care because I couldn't do anything for myself. I couldn't even go the bathroom alone.

My daughter, being a therapist herself, thought, "Oh, my God, we have to get my Mother over her fear of stairs." So, she called someone. That was the beginning of my working with a local therapist. It was wonderful. It helped me get over the Post-Traumatic Stress Disorder of stairs.

It was a *long* recovery. I had months of physical therapy. They said I might not ever get back full use of my arm. But I met the challenge. Today I have full range of motion.

Something terrible turned into something I learned from. With the right medical care, the right recovery, the right attitude, the right therapist. It could have been much worse. They thought I was going to die in the ER.

During her recovery, Lindy found that the pain medications she had been prescribed made her vomit. And vomiting hurt her arm and shoulder. She argued with the home-health care nurse, who insisted that she needed to keep her pain under control.

It was then that she began to take control of her own medical care. She spoke to her pharmacist about the side effects of her medication. He suggested she speak with her doctor about another alternative, one that often had fewer side effects. She did. The doctor agreed. It worked.

She also learned how to text and play video games left-handed on her phone. That lesson, she assures us, had limited utility.

Finally, Lindy learned during this long recovery to accept help.

- Assemble your friends and family. They want to help you. They want to be part of your recovery. You have to learn to let them.
- Learn to ask for what you need. Friends can help both you and your primary caregiver. They can be cheerleaders – urging you on. They can be baby-sitters for you when you can't be left alone. They can be chauffeurs when you can't drive. (God, I couldn't drive for nearly a year!) They can step in just when you need it. And they often do.

- Teach them to make specific offers: "Would you like me to drive you to PT? May I bring you dinner?" Those questions are much better than "Can I do anything for you?"

This first speed bump prepared Lindy for the others she was soon to encounter. And it headed her down the path of developing her own set of guidelines:

- Be organized. Garlic Fest was a success even without me because of my clipboard.
- Slow down. Appreciate life.
- Live every day.
- Take vacations.
- Look for balance.
- Find what gives you joy and surround yourself with it.

# Second Bump

## Kevin's Cancer

After returning home from a vacation in Italy in June, 2013, Kevin, Lindy's husband, began showing signs of gastric distress. Their first thoughts were that he had picked up a traveler's bug, but when his weight loss began to get serious, Lindy insisted that he see a gastroenterologist. The initial tests were all negative, but Lindy insisted that something was wrong. The doctor ordered a colonoscopy.

> It was very interesting, medically, because all of his colonoscopies had been negative. Not even a darned polyp. And I was always jealous. I asked why he should get a colonoscopy. He was on a ten-year schedule. He had had one five years before. But the doctor said it was the next step.

I had been convinced that there was nothing wrong. On July 2, 2013, we saw the doctor for the results. I was holding my grandchild in my arms when the doctor told us, "I cannot believe the size of the tumor. I don't even need to biopsy it to know that it's cancer." I nearly dropped the baby in the floor. My husband took it extremely well. I did not.

The doctor calmly told us that this kind of surgery wasn't performed in Bennington, so we had to do some research and make some decisions. I started talking to friends and contacts. We have a friend who knew someone who had had the same kind of surgery at Memorial Sloan Kettering, so I went through the process of getting him accepted by the tumor board: sending slides, etc.

We got accepted. But my husband gave me a very hard time. We owned the restaurant, still, and he wanted to do his treatment some place closer. Like Albany. But I said, "We are going to the best! And the doctor at Sloan Kettering was one of the top three in the world." He wouldn't agree.

I was shopping at Midnight Madness when I ran into a friend who had been a nurse practitioner. I told her the situation. She immediately went to my house and gave Kevin a chewing out. By the time I got home, he said "We're going to New York." It was the best decision of our lives.

During the time that Lindy and Kevin owned Kevin's Sports Bar and Restaurant, they always had a huge Customer Appreciation Picnic on the Fourth of July, but just after learning about Kevin's cancer, Lindy was not handling the news very well. In addition, she had a new grandchild about to be born on Cape Cod.

> So, I called friends, my mother, and my sister, and handed each of them a clipboard with assigned tasks and said, "I am running away. I'm going to do something positive. I am going to see this baby born." I can't believe to this day that I did that. But I did! And it was just the strength and energy I needed to go on and fight the battle. I needed something joyful!"

The treatments at Sloan Kettering began in August. Kevin received chemo right away. Because he was originally from Blue Point, Long Island, his medical team set him up for treatment at a satellite unit in Commack, Long Island, near his hometown, where all his family lives.

> That was a good decision. We could stay overnight with his family, and he had friends and family to support him. We went down and back or stayed overnight for his chemo treatments for several months. He did very well with chemo. He even went to work a few times with this chemo in a fanny pack. It was a struggle but we got through it.

On New Year's Eve, he started radiation treatment in Commack. He had to live there, since he had treatments every day. I would go down with him on the train, drop him off, and go back to pick him up. We did that for several months.

He did very well with the radiation, too. He stayed at one of his brothers' houses, and he was able to get up and cook and do many other things. He kind of enjoyed being with his family during that time.

The chemo and radiation had shrunk the tumor so that they could remove it. They scheduled the surgery for the end of March, 2014. That was a tough time. It was major surgery. Going in, we didn't know if he would end up with a temporary or life-long colostomy bag. You just have to wait and see what happens.

Luckily, the robotic surgery went well. Kevin ended up with only a very small incision and no colostomy bag, but it was very painful for him. He was on a morphine drip, and they were having a difficult time getting him off it since he was in so much pain.

That was when I had a big teaching moment at Sloan. I went to their Integrative Medicine place on 72$^{nd}$ street and told them, "I need acupuncture on my husband right now!" Within hours, he was off the morphine. Everyone around the bed, even the surgeon, said, "OK, what just happened?" I told them it was something they needed to be aware of – Acupuncture.

Next, a very old-fashioned drug, gabapentin, for nerve pain, had helped him during radiation. I suggested we try it for surgical pain. The surgeon had never heard of it, but he agreed to try. And between the acupuncture and the gabapentin, it was a miracle!

Recovery from the surgery was not fast, but by the annual July 4 picnic in 2014, Lindy and Kevin were ready to celebrate. They called it the Freedom from Cancer celebration and got t-shirts for everyone to help them celebrate.

Doctors are not quick to announce a cure, but after many follow-up tests and colonoscopies, they officially declared Kevin cancer-free two years later in July, 2016.

I am grateful every time I go with Kevin for his check-ups. He always gets good reports. I almost get jealous, because I never get a good one. I think my husband has a little guilt that he is cured.

Ever one to look for the lesson, Lindy said she was able to use what she learned from her accident and recovery to help her with Kevin's journey.

I learned empathy after being through the shoulder experience. And I think my experience gave Kevin hope. I got better; he could, too.

And of course, there were new lessons to be learned as a caregiver during Kevin's illness and recovery:

- Rally the troops. I learned how to be a cheerleader and how to rally the troops to be cheerleaders, too. You just can't go through this alone.
- Find whatever brings you joy. Make sure it happens. Once when Kevin was not progressing as fast as he might, I taped up pictures of the grandkids at the end of his bed, and told him, "That's what you're living for. That joy!"
- Think outside the box. Go to Plan B when something isn't working. And push your doctors to go to Plan B, too.
- Speak up. If you can't speak up for yourself, find a family member or friend who will. You may need to scream and yell and threaten to call the governor if you can't get what you need.
- Get on a five-year schedule for colonoscopies. Even if you don't get polyps, a lot can happen in five years!

Another theme that Lindy frequently returns to is that of the need for a Medical Navigator.

What hospitals call a Patient Advocate and what I do are very different things. They just hold your hand and point you to various resources. They don't really help you know which steps to take first.

Doctors and nurses don't always have the time to help people through the process. We need more volunteers to do it. They need to be there in the Cancer Center with the information that patients need.

Even places like Sloan don't have as much as they should. They called a social worker for me. I didn't need a social worker; I needed a Navigator. I had to blaze my own trail.

Life's speed bumps slow us down, help us to learn lessons we need, but often come at what seem to be the most unbelievable times.

# More Bumps Ahead

## It Started with Breast Cancer

Kevin's celebration party was on July 4, 2014. It looked like Kevin and Lindy were out of the woods. About three weeks after the party, one of their employees was worried about going for her first mammogram and discussed it with Lindy.

> Just by coincidence, I noticed that I had my own mammogram scheduled two days later, on July 31. So, I decided to do a self-exam before I went. And sure enough, I felt a lump. I thought, "You have got to be kidding me!" I started to panic a little, but I remembered that I had had negative lumps before, and I was going in for the exam the very next day.

I went in for my normal, scheduled exam. They called back that afternoon. The navigator said they didn't see anything on the side where the lump was, but they saw some things on the right side.

I said, "Well, something's wrong with this picture because this is a palpable lump. Something has to be done."

I went to my primary right away, and she agreed. She scheduled me for an ultrasound later that week. After that test, the breast navigator called me and said they were seeing suspicious things in BOTH breasts.

I was getting a little panicky. I went back to my primary to say we have got to do something, fast.

Lindy's primary physician tried to schedule her for biopsies at Dartmouth, but they couldn't get her in for several weeks.

Then I thought about the great experience we had had with Kevin at Memorial Sloan Kettering, and I decided to see if I could get an appointment there. My primary doctor agreed.

I made appointments at Sloan and started the panic attacks, the sadness, and everything that goes with it thinking, "Are you kidding? We only had a three-week break."

I went for the biopsies on August 13, 2014. They were pure hell. I remember lying there, screaming in pain when one of the doctors above me said, "Ah, she's a redhead. She needs more medicine." And I couldn't have epinephrine because I have palpitations.

That was a little speed bump, just getting the biopsies.

That night, while staying in New York, Lindy and Kevin continued a practice they had begun with Kevin's treatment. They tried to do something fun and exciting while they were in the city. This time, Lindy thought that being near water would calm her, so a cruise on the Hudson filled their evening.

The next day, they were in a restaurant when the call came in: positive on the left; benign on the right.

I had a nervous breakdown in the restaurant, ran out without paying, and decided I needed to be somewhere quiet where I could think and pray. I screamed like a psychopath at the cab driver to take me to St. Patrick's Cathedral. He did. Quickly.

I prayed. I took deep breaths, I tried to get my life back together. I called my contact at Sloan and asked if it was possible for me to meet with the surgeon the next day so I could go home with information.

Luckily, Lindy had used a workbook, ***Difficult Conversations***, that helped her formulate questions to ask her new doctor.

She met her new surgeon, who laid out all the options: lumpectomy, mastectomy, chemotherapy, radiation, the whole gamut of possibilities. She and Kevin went home that night with a lot of information and an equal amount of stress. Lindy gave her news to family and friends and launched her new research project into breast cancer. She chose to have a lumpectomy.

After setting the date for surgery, she had to go back to Sloan for a pre-op procedure where they inserted a radioactive material used to locate the sentinel node, a lymph node that is an early indicator of a metastasized tumor.

> The night before the pre-op, Kevin and I went to a Billy Joel concert at Madison Square Garden and stayed out much too late. It was terrific, but I don't suggest staying up so late before a pre-op.

# MRSA

And then the surgery.

So here we go for the BIG surgery of a lumpectomy. I went home the next day, wrapped up like a mummy. Two days later, my mother and Kevin were babysitting me, and I didn't feel well.

Here's another example of how I know my body and how I pay attention. That's saved me many, many times during this journey. Knowing what to look for, being a nurse, paying attention.

My mother said, "Of course you don't feel well. You just had surgery."

But I said, "No. Something's up." I went and took my temperature, and sure enough, it was 102. I said, "We've got to get this bandage off! We've got to get this off right now!"

I started to panic. My husband thought I was overreacting. But we finally got the bandage off, and I could see I had a big infection.

I took a picture and sent it to Sloan. They said I had to get to the ER immediately. So many people don't pay attention to infections, and it turns into staph. That's why people die, sometimes. They don't look at their wounds early enough.

So, I knew. I knew I was in trouble. I went to the SVMC ER with my husband and my mother, who were my "private duty nurses" beginning with this trip.

It was a full-blown infection. They admitted me into the hospital for another horrible stint. I was in the hospital for eleven days. I had sepsis, staph, and MRSA [Methicillin-resistant Staphylococcus aureus, a very hard to treat strain of staph].

That was a nightmare, but it was my first encounter with Dr. Salem, who has been my surgeon ever since. And my first encounter with Dr. George, the Infection Control Officer. We've been seeing each other since then, too.

That little bitty incision for the lumpectomy blew up with the staph and MRSA. Then they had to open it to drain it. I ended up with a huge incision by the time I left the hospital.

That was another speed bump.

Lindy had been scheduled to start chemotherapy after the lumpectomy, but that had to be delayed because of the infections. When she did get home, it was under the care of a home-health nurse.

It was the beginning of my experience with every-day torture to get the wound healed.

While in the hospital, Lindy had her first experience with Reiki, a type of healing touch therapy. SVMC has a group of Reiki practitioners who volunteer their time to help patients with pain and healing. She continued Reiki and regular visits with her therapist after leaving the hospital.

I was having trouble with pain meds and being sick all the time. I lost twenty pounds, but I gained it back ten minutes later! And I took a sabbatical from work and the Chamber [of Commerce].

I just had to stay at home and heal. I felt very private. Usually, I'm not; but then I didn't want to be around people. I just hunkered down and tried to get through the nightmare.

## Chemo

Once the wound was fully healed, Lindy needed to decide where she wanted to have her chemo. Her primary physician strongly recommended having it in Bennington to save her from having to travel to New York.

She wanted to do her chemo and radiation in the same place. She interviewed both at SVMC and at Sloan, but she chose to go to Sloan because SVMC, at that time, did not have a single-beam radiation machine.

On November 1, 2014, Lindy's friends put on a fund-raiser over her objections. They wanted to do it as encouragement for her. It was a humbling and surprising experience for Lindy and a complete success. Hundreds of people attended and donated. A Go-Fund-Me campaign raised even more money. Lindy used it to help with all the train trips and New York hotels.

On December 16, 2014, I had my first chemo, scared to death because they tell you everything that can happen to you. I tolerated chemo OK. It made me weak and tired. And the morning following chemo, I had to get a shot of Neulasta to increase my white blood cell count. I always stayed overnight for the shot after the chemo.

The main side effect of the Neulasta shot was bone pain. I thought I was dying. The pain was like being shot with a paint gun. You didn't know where you were going to get it. It's shooting in your arm! It's shooting in your leg! It was just hell! Hell! Hell! Hell!

I had to go for chemo every three weeks. I had some of the side effects. Not as many as some do. Not the vomiting. I had more shakiness and tiredness. I still had my appetite. I told the aides who took my weight each time I went in that one thing I wanted was to lose weight, but they said, "Oh, no, no, no! Those skinny girls don't do so well. You don't want to lose weight now."

When Lindy's hair began falling out, she had to decide when and how much to cut it.

Normally, I'm not a vain person, but cutting my hair was horrible. I cried my eyes out. I had to do it, but I didn't want to. So, I cut it really short and got a wig here and another one in New York. Then I got a buzz cut.

I surprised myself at how it affected me. I never let anyone see me without my wig. In fact, I couldn't even look at myself in the mirror without it on. It said "sickness" to me.

But everyone loved my wigs. Looking at the pictures now, my wigs looked really good, but then it was tough. But I got through it.

As she continued chemo, Lindy added more and more alternative and integrative treatments to her regime: massages, Reiki, and acupuncture as well as continued therapy.

> I wrote in my journal, "Chemo is kicking my butt." I went through a lot of anger. The one thing that really helped was acupuncture. When I got home from a session, Kevin would bring me to acupuncture, and I'd come out wanting to get a sandwich at Subway. Acupuncture was amazingly, spontaneously wonderful during chemo. At other times I didn't really see the benefit for a little while, but during chemo it was immediately effective.

Because of the lumpectomy on Lindy's left side, the chemo could only be started in veins on her right side, and a port was not possible because of the MRSA. As the treatments continued, the veins on the right began to collapse, so that she felt like a pincushion each time she got a treatment.

She was tired. She slept a lot. She had a stuffy nose. She coughed. If there was a side effect listed anywhere, she got it. But she kept telling herself that each treatment improved her chances for good things to happen. And she and Kevin continued trying to do something fun the night before a treatment.

> We would go to a good restaurant, try to do something joyful. I would post it on Facebook and read the comments. We saw six plays. We had unbelievable meals. We went to parades. You can always find something good to balance something bad.

A chaplain in the breast cancer center helped her get through the process by sitting with her during the treatment. The chaplain also suggested that Lindy's family could better understand what she was going through if they accompanied her.

> I didn't want my mother to. I thought it would be too much for her. But I made my daughter go on the chemo floor with me. She had no idea! But it turned her into one of my best supporters and encouragers.

Halfway through the treatment, they changed the chemo drugs. The new one had even more side effects, including a very odd one.

> It made your toenails and fingernails fall off. One of the nurses told me to soak my fingers and toes in ice water during the treatment, and I wouldn't lose my nails. I did that. I didn't lose my nails.
>
> By the sixth treatment, I was having severe bone pain and was having to take pain meds. But because my pharmacist suggested Tramadol during my shoulder episode, I wasn't sick to my stomach. It's important to have a pharmacist on your team!

After one of the treatments, Lindy got a touch of pneumonia and spent a night in the hospital. But nothing terribly serious happened until February, 2015, when with her redhead's sensitive skin, she developed a Chemo Rash.

> My doctor sent me to the dermatologist at Sloan because they have fabulous creams to stop the itching. The doctor looked over my entire body as he was examining the rash, and when he got to my foot all hell broke loose!
>
> People started coming in, taking pictures, and I realized something must be wrong with my foot.
>
> I yelled, "You better get my husband in here! I'm having a panic attack!"
>
> The doctor said, "It looks like melanoma."
>
> I said, "What? I'm in the middle of chemo and you're going to tell me that?"
>
> We took the train home, scared to death, and waited to hear the results.

## Melanoma

After a biopsy, the test results confirmed what the dermatologist had suspected. Lindy had acral lentiginous melanoma (ALM) on her heel.

I never noticed it. Earlier, my masseuse had said my heel looked stained, and I thought maybe I just wasn't washing my feet well enough. Being a redhead, I always paid attention to all the charts showing skin cancers, but when I looked at my heel, I didn't see anything alarming, just a little discoloration. But the biopsy was positive.

So, then I had to research this melanoma. I found out it was rare, and often fatal. I was depressed again, feeling like I had been slammed to the ground. Again.

I had to meet with the melanoma surgeon. He said I could wait until I finished the chemo for my breast cancer before I needed to have the melanoma surgery.

I finished my chemo in March, 2015, and I kept a promise to myself. I went to Good Morning America and held a big sign that said "I finished my chemo and I'd love to meet Robin Roberts." And I got picked to go in to the show! I was on TV with her for just a little bit. She said, "She's a warrior, and I'm a warrior." It was very cool. I met my goal before my next battle.

One of Lindy's nurses at Sloan was part of an organization rather like Make-A-Wish. She put in for Lindy and Kevin to have an all-expenses-paid vacation at the beach in Florida before Lindy had to begin radiation for the breast cancer and surgery for the melanoma.

> My first thought was, "I'm dying. That's why she did this." But she said no, she was only trying to give me a break. It was wonderful.

In April, 2015, Lindy had already had a few radiation treatments before the surgery on her foot. As with the breast, they did sentinel node mapping.

> We had no idea how bad the surgery was going to be. It wasn't just my foot. It was abdominal surgery, too, to remove the sentinel nodes from my groin. And they hadn't realized how deep my nodes are in my abdomen.
>
> They were going to send me home the next day, but my husband said, "Are you kidding? She can't even lift up in the bed!"
>
> Luckily, we had a little apartment in a building that was associated with New York Presbyterian Hospital, so I stayed there. I had a huge wound bag, I was in a wheelchair, and we had to live in that little apartment because I still had to do the radiation for breast cancer. Even with all that mess attached to me. It was awful.

Being in a wheelchair is a whole new experience to begin with. Then there were the pain levels and the wound care to deal with.

On my birthday, May 20, 2015, I finished the radiation. And as we had done before, we celebrated by doing something I had always wanted to do: buy a bottle of Dom Perignon and tour the city in a limo since I was still in a wheelchair.

## Skin Graft

Six days later, on May 26, 2015, Lindy had a skin graft from her thigh to replace her heel that had been totally removed.

> Now I've got a piece of my thigh gone. And in order for the graft to work, I couldn't get out of bed except for the commode.
>
> I learned to play a lot of cards. My daughter called some of my friends and relatives to come stay overnight with me so Kevin could have a break.
>
> I had to have wound care every day. The nurse would debride the wound. I had to bite on a piece of wood or a folded washcloth to endure the pain. It was the most excruciating pain I've ever lived through.
>
> I thought about jumping out the window.
>
> I was pushed around in a wheelchair. Once my daughter was pushing me while wearing flip-flops and almost tipped me over in a puddle. And my son pushed me through Central Park Zoo, but got so enamored of taking pictures of the animals, he forgot to set the break and I went rolling down a hill.
>
> I learned a lot about wheelchair accessibility while we were in New York. Many restaurants advertised that they were, but when we got there we couldn't get in. I gained a lot of empathy for people who have to use a wheelchair.

After about six weeks, Lindy got to go home with her round-the-clock caregivers, her husband and mother. Once there, she had to crawl up the steps into her house on her knees. And she wasn't very interested in leaving. She had gotten so weak from lack of activity that she hired a trainer to help her with upper-body exercises so she could regain her strength.

In early July, 2015, Lindy met her new Melanoma Oncology doctor. He had just opened a practice at Sloan. Maybe that helps explain the misunderstanding:

> I didn't take good notes at our first meeting. I just cried my eyes out, and I didn't really hear him. That's why you need to take a recorder with you.
>
> I thought he said I only had a year to live. I cried and cried and said I was not leaving New York without getting in to see him again.
>
> I got back in. He apologized. What he meant was that if I had gotten this before 2009, before all the miracle drugs, people were not living more than a year. And he said it is a deadly disease, but there are all kinds of things that could happen.
>
> I felt a little more optimistic at that point.
>
> Each time I saw him, I had to have either an ultrasound or a CT scan because there was one node in my right groin that he was suspicious of. He took a needle biopsy that was negative, but he still didn't like the looks of it.

I went for scans every three months, and everything was going well.

In October, 2015, Lindy had her Breast Cancer Survivor Party, inviting all those who had helped her through that journey. The party theme was the Survivor television series, but the biggest event was the wig-burning and Lindy's showing off her very short curls.

Determined to enjoy her period of well-being, Lindy planned activities to bring her joy.

On January 1, 2016, my months-long planning paid off when I took my mother and my granddaughter to DisneyWorld. That is a joyous memory I will hold in my heart forever!

May 20, 2016, was my 60th birthday. I spent a couple of months planning a magical birthday party at the Equinox in Manchester. Every birthday is important. Sixty is an important milestone. But when you've been diagnosed with these illnesses, birthdays are even more important. I wasn't going to risk anyone else planning my party.

With the help of my family, I planned it. 60 people, chocolate fountains, Julie Shea band. I did it up, and did it up well! The lesson here is Don't Wait! Party it up!

My husband gave me a birthday present that met a lifelong goal: a trip to Alaska. I still use my memories of looking at those animals in my meditation today. It was the most exciting trip I have ever been on in my life.

Almost exactly two years after discovering the lump in her breast, in August, 2016, Lindy begins experiencing pain in her groin.

Sometimes members of the team have different opinions. My oncologist said he was not liking the look of it, but we could wait and watch. It had grown two millimeters since the last exam. Then I asked my surgeon, who said, "There's a 20% chance that it's not good."

I made the decision. I said, "I'm not good with odds. Let's get a biopsy."

In November, 2016, I had the biopsy. It was positive for melanoma.

Right after the biopsy, I decided to run away again. We decided to go somewhere we'd never been. So, we went to the Outer Banks of North Carolina, and we did a lot of soul-searching.

I have used this lesson – always get a second opinion – in helping others decide what to do. If I hadn't asked the surgeon for his opinion, too, I might have waited too late.

# Radical Lymph Node Dissection

Lindy's next surgery at Sloan was one she never wanted to have to do. On December 3, 2016, she had a total radical lymph node dissection of the nodes in her right groin. Her leg would never be the same: she would have lifetime lymphedema, a swelling of the affected leg because of blockage of the lymph system by removal of lymph nodes.

But she had to do it to save her life.

> That was a horrible surgery. I thought I was going to die. I was in the hospital for quite a few days. I had tons of tubes in my leg. And it was Christmastime.
>
> Kevin was there, trying to stay in a hotel, and he didn't tell me but he had to change hotel rooms every night because all the hotels were filled with Christmas travelers. He brought his little suitcase in with him every day. The security guards at the hospital finally asked him if he was homeless. He told them he felt like he was.
>
> Really the only good thing about having had MRSA was that I got a private room when it was active. But by this surgery, the MRSA was gone. I had to share a room. That was awful.
>
> I finally got home on December 10, but good care was critical. I had to have home health nurses watching the wound. And with the drains, I was back to being barely able to walk.

Once again, I needed round-the-clock care, provided by my family. I swear to God that my husband was a saint. He had to change all those drains!

All my family was terrific in helping me get through this. And it wasn't just one time. It was numerous times! I'm sure they were all saying, "Oh, my God, is this ever going to end?"

It was close to Christmas. All of the family had come for a big celebration. Lindy's friends came and decorated her house for the season. She was recuperating, and decided she really wanted to go to church on Christmas Eve.

I was feeling a little short of breath, but I thought it was only because I hadn't been up very much.

I woke up Christmas morning and was not feeling well. I got through the day, opened my presents, but I knew something was wrong. I couldn't take a deep breath. I thought I might have a blood clot.

I called my local surgeon. He said, "You have to go in. You know that. I know you know that."

I admitted that I did.

Kevin was about to cook dinner for all the family. I told him that he was not taking me to the ER. He was going to stay home and cook Christmas dinner the way I would want it, and my mother would take me. She could eat her dinner when she was done.

As it turned out, we both had Christmas dinner a month later.

## Pulmonary Embolism and Cellulitis

At the SVMC ER, the doctors had a discussion which Lindy overheard, that they were not prepared to deal with such a serious condition and should MedFlight her to another hospital. She thought she was about to die. Again.

But cooler heads took control. They put her on blood thinners for the numerous blood clots they found in her lungs, and put her in intensive care on Christmas night.

Two days later, she came home.

> I was still recovering from everything. I had severe lymphedema in my leg, and I couldn't even go to lymphedema training because of the blood clots.

Things calmed down. Lindy finally got to go to training in how to deal with her lymphedema in March, 2017.

> Let me tell you, lymphedema is a fricking nightmare. The wrapping, from my toes up! Having to have my husband learn how to do it. I couldn't walk. I was wrapped like a mummy. But I had to do it to get the swelling down.

I remember sitting there, when I was at physical therapy. It was horrible! But if you do it, if you keep it up, you can get back to normal size. I still have to do it. Every night I wrap my leg in a pressure quilt. Managing lymphedema is a life-long process. You never cure it but you can manage it.

Then in April, she was back in the hospital at SVMC for three days with cellulitis, a bacterial infection of the skin that was likely related to the lymphedema, and was particularly dangerous because of her missing lymph nodes.

During the next several months, life continued without drama. Lindy started physical therapy. She had regular scans, and all was going well.

True to her practice, Lindy used this calm to promote joy in her life. For her birthday in May, 2017, she swam with the dolphins in Miami.

I met another goal. When you're feeling good, you've got to jump out with your parachute and have fun!

In July, 2017, I thought it was time for my husband to fulfil a goal. He always wanted to go to Cubs Stadium, so we went to Chicago, toured Chicago, and he got to go to a Cubs game.

In October, 2017, she got both a clear mammogram and a clear brain scan. To celebrate that they went to San Francisco and Lake Tahoe in November. And the spot of skin cancer they found in December, 2017, was only basal cell carcinoma, which was successfully removed.

## Metastasized Melanoma

Then in January, 2018, they found three more spots of melanoma during a regularly scheduled CT scan. It had metastasized. That placed her in Stage 4, where she was eligible for immunotherapy.

In February, 2018, I started my first dose of immunotherapy, Keytruda. You've probably seen it on television. It works for everybody but me. It cured Jimmy Carter's brain cancer. My doctor even said, "I hope that guy doesn't die right away. All my patients are watching Jimmy Carter!"

I had infusions in February, March, and April, 2018. It works like chemo in many ways.

Then in April, 2018, I got devastating news. The first scan showed the Keytruda was not touching my tumors. They were not shrinking.

I thought again about jumping out the window. It was reasonable: I was on the tenth floor, and I couldn't take any more bad news. I cried and told the doctor he could never bring me bad news again. He said there was still hope – other choices, other drugs. I continued taking Keytruda until June with no side effects.

On July 25, 2018, I got my first treatment with two new drugs: Opdivo and Yervoy [combined immunotherapy for advanced melanoma that activates the immune system against cancer]. We knew going in that this new treatment had an unbelievable number of side effects. And we knew that I get them.

In August, I ended up at the SVMC ER twice for infections in my leg. Each time I got a fancier antibiotic. Then I got a rash that continued to worsen until I had to call Sloan. That put me in the hospital at SVMC for two days because of the hives and severe reaction to the antibiotics. But Garlic Fest still happened.

In September, 2018, I missed my second treatment because I was still suffering from side effects: colitis, diarrhea, weight loss, weakness, severe rash, and depression. A tough month.

I continued to use Integrative and Alternative therapies during September but with not as much success as in the past.

A CT scan in mid-September revealed blood clots in my lungs, adding a life-long blood thinner to my medications. They found a new spot on my liver, but all the metastasized spots were stable.

## Current Status

As this book is completed in late October, 2018, Lindy has stopped the immunotherapy infusions at Sloan Kettering since they had not been effective. Each treatment had left her facing a set of varying side effects from which she had to recover, often including a trip to the emergency room or a hospital stay.

Beginning in early November, she will enter a clinical trial of a new immunotherapy drug, also at Sloan Kettering. Lindy is not quitting. The journey continues.

She will also continue for the next six years to take tamoxifen, the breast cancer drug which revolutionized breast cancer treatment when it was first introduced over forty years ago.

She leads or participates in community activities. She speaks at health forums about her experiences with the health care system, and her team-approach to healing. She willingly shares her strategies and lessons-learned with anyone who comes to her for guidance or comfort.

She inspires everyone who knows her to fight on, live their lives, and find their joy.

# Navigating the System

# Lessons Learned

Throughout Lindy's four-year journey with cancer, its treatments and their side effects, she had been keeping a journal, tracking things she learned and wanted to share with others.

The same themes that came up during Kevin's cancer and Lindy's shoulder injury recur and are deepened as she learns more about the medical system and her own capabilities.

- Use Integrated and Alternative Care. I used everything I could find: Reiki, acupuncture, massage, meditation, therapy.

- Build a Team. This time I needed a full team: my primary physician who was the glue to hold the rest together; the pharmacist; the therapist; the acupuncturist; the Reiki master; the minister; the personal trainer; the Angel Cards reader [Angel Cards are rather like Tarot cards and used similarly], and many others.

- Be Organized. I have notebooks I carry with me to every appointment filled with questions, their answers, and follow-up questions.

- Be Assertive. Ask for, even demand, what you need from appointment schedulers, insurance companies, financial offices. My lawyer said it is better to ask for forgiveness than permission. I had to fight hard to get my first immunotherapy, including calling the president of Blue Cross. Also, doctors are not gods. Stand up to them and question what they recommend.

- Learn Patience. I am shocked at myself that I made it through having to be in bed and not moving, being in the wheelchair, and being slammed to the ground over and over with bad news and getting back up.

- Gather Cheerleaders. I needed all my friends and family not giving up, cheering me on. FaceBook friends I never met cheering me on. My grandchildren, their pictures, their smiles, their videos cheering me on.

- Be Public about Illness. I chose to be public, to talk about it, to post information on Facebook. It helped me not feel alone, and I hope it can help others learn from my journey.

- Pray. I have always been spiritual rather than religious. I had an experience when I thought I was dying. I saw the light, the whole nine yards. I developed a relationship with the minister of the local Congregational Church, who helped me to feel the strength of prayer.

- Read Angel Cards. Throughout this process my gifted Angel reader has given me hope and positive thoughts to hold onto.

- Use All the Tools. Meditation tapes and soft music help me relax and sleep. Drugs are not the only thing that help, but they also should be used when needed.

- Meet with a Therapist. I learned so much from her when I got slapped down. I learned about Post-Traumatic Stress Disorder and ways to deal with it. I learned a mantra: "Feelings are like ocean waves." They should be allowed to be felt, then let go. You need to feel sad. Feel it and let it go. You need to feel angry. Feel it and let it go. You need to feel joy. Feel it and try to hold on to it a little longer.

- Be a Personal Health Advocate. I am public with my illness. Others know what I have gone through. They ask for help and guidance, and I tell them what I've learned. Kevin does the same.

- Avoid Overload. It's easy to get too much information, too much advice, too many appointments. You need to find balance. Balance integrative and traditional medicine, chemicals and spirituality. Don't only be a patient; live your life, too.

- Be Smart. I learned to pay attention to my body. If I don't feel comfortable with what a doctor says, I get a second opinion.

- Find and Surround Yourself with Joy. Celebrate anything you can. Reward yourself for completing hard tasks. Cheer yourself up before hard decisions. Enjoy yourself when you feel good. Grab onto happiness. Do something good to balance the bad.

# Preparing to Visit Your Doctor

- Research your doctor and medical center. Ask for references. Start with Google and gather the evidence. Look at your doctor's statistics, such as number of successful surgeries, to help you judge experience levels. Consider the location and whether travel to a distant site is your best option.

- Keep a notebook or a journal. Before you visit your doctor, make a list of questions that you want answered. Then don't leave until you get complete answers. Write down everything and keep it to refer to for subsequent visits.

- Research your diagnosis to find questions others have asked. Add them to your list.

- Bring another set of ears and/or a voice recorder with you to your appointments. Sometimes I got so upset, I forgot to listen.

- Don't be intimidated by the doctors. Insist they answer your questions so that you understand. Teach your doctor how to communicate with you.

# Dealing with Insurance Companies

- One of the best things I did was to buy Cancer Insurance from a hard-pressing representative of that silly duck.  Having that extra money has made the difference in my recovery. It relieved financial stress and let me have the good and joyful moments to balance the awful ones of treatment. The return on that investment has been incredible.

- I have said it before: "Ask for forgiveness rather than for permission." If you get a denial, don't settle for "No" when you need a different medication or treatment than the insurance company wants to pay for. Push every way you can.

- Read the fine print on your insurance policy. Be sure you understand the limitations on things like "out of network" and how those will affect you financially.

- Look into options for additional insurance even after a diagnosis:  life insurance may still be a possibility.

## Managing Survivor Guilt

As you move through the system of cancer treatment, you often make friends with fellow travelers. When one passes away, you may have to deal with feelings of guilt that you have survived.

During my journey, I have attended the funerals of eight of my friends. As I sat through their services, I kept wondering how it is that I have survived when they have not.

Even though these feelings may be irrational, they are very real. I believe that we need to deal with them. I have gotten through them by working with a therapist, and using the spiritual practices of prayer and acknowledging my blessings.

# Planning for End-of-Life

I have come to realize that I need to force the issue of planning for my end-of-life. I have been to the funeral home, I bought a cemetery plot, and I am writing down how I want things to be.

I don't think it's fair to leave these things undone and expect my family to make all the decisions. Most families don't want to discuss these "morbid" issues, but making them guess about what a family member wants when it's too late to ask is much worse.

I am also starting a Grandmother Scrapbook for each of my grandchildren with photos and letters for them to read later.

# Integrative and Alternative Medicine

Integrative Medicine is a form of medical therapy that combines practices and treatments from alternative and complementary medicine with conventional medicine. Rather than encouraging patients to use only traditional, western, allopathic treatments, or only non-mainstream alternative medical treatments, Integrative Medicine incorporates complementary techniques into specialized care for each individual patient.

Lindy has incorporated many alternative and complementary practices into her healing regimen including those listed below preceded by an asterisk (*).

**\*Acupuncture** is a treatment in which thin needles are inserted into the body along energy or chi meridians. It is a key component of traditional Chinese medicine and is primarily used for pain control and wellness balancing.

**\*Alternate Medical Systems**
- **\*Chiropractic Medicine** focuses on disorders of the musculoskeletal system (primarily the spine) and the nervous system, and the effects of these disorders on general health.
- **\*Homeopathy** is based on the belief that the body can cure itself through the use of tiny amounts of natural substances, like plants and minerals, that can stimulate the healing process based on the doctrine of "like cures like.

- **Naturopathy** is based on the theory that diseases can be successfully treated or prevented without the use of drugs, by using techniques such as control of diet, exercise, and massage

- **Osteopathic Medicine** focuses on the joints, muscles, and spine to positively affect the body's nervous, circulatory, and lymphatic systems.

*\*Aromatherepy* uses scents from natural plant extracts to stimulate health and well-being.

**\*Biofeedback Therapy** is a technique that trains people to improve their health by controlling certain bodily processes that normally happen involuntarily, such as heart rate, blood pressure, muscle tension, and skin temperature.

**\*Card Reading** is a way of obtaining messages about the present and future using cards from specialized decks such as the Tarot, Angel Tarot, and Oracle cards.

**\*Counseling/Therapy** is based on the core idea that talking about the things that are bothering you can help clarify them and put them in perspective.

**\*Massage Therapy** consists of many techniques from many traditions all based generally on the process of rubbing, kneading, vibrating, or tapping muscles to make them feel better.

**\*Nutrition Counseling** helps develop dietary plans for individuals with particular medical conditions or for generalized well-being.

**\*Natural Products and Supplements** may be very helpful in increasing wellness without adding prescription medicines, but must be monitored carefully to ensure that they do not adversely interact with each other or with prescribed medications.

**\*Reiki** is a Japanese healing technique based on the principle that the therapist can channel energy into the patient by means of touch, laying on of hands, to activate the natural healing processes of the patient's body and restore physical and emotional well-being.

\***Reflexology** is the application of appropriate pressure to specific points and areas on the feet, hands, or ears that correspond to different body organs and systems.

**\*Relaxation and Movement** techniques come from many traditions but all have goals of stress reduction, pain reduction, and feeling of peace and well-being.

> \*Breathing Exercise
> \*Guided Imagery
> Hypnotherapy
> Pilates
> \*Progressive Muscle Relaxation
> Qi Gong
> Tai Chi
> \*Yoga

## Traditional Healing

*Ayurvedic Medicine

*Shamanic Medicine

*Traditional Chinese Medicine

# Organizations That Can Help

Many local and national organizations provide support services to those of us with cancer.

In Bennington, Vermont, many of these organizations have supported me:

**Bennington Holistic Healing Practitioners** is a group of integrative and holistic practitioners who have joined together to better serve the community.

(http://bennhhp.org/)

**Cancer Center Community Crusaders,** "The4Cs," provide financial, physical, and emotional support to members of the community and their families as they strive to obtain the best cancer care and treatment possible.

( http://www.facebook.com/CCCCrusaders)

**Speak Sooner at the Center for Communications in Medicine** has as its mission to educate patients, families and healthcare professionals about the key role of communication in improving healthcare delivery.

(http://www.speaksooner.org/)

**Southwestern Vermont Regional Cancer Center** provides a full spectrum of support services to cancer patients in conjunction with Southwestern Vermont Medical Center. Services include Reiki, yoga sessions, and wig and makeup consultations.

(http://svhealthcare.org/services/cancer-center/)

For anyone traveling within New York State, Amtrak has a program called **Rails to Recovery** that provides a free companion ticket for anyone traveling to receive treatment for life-threatening illness.

Also, Amtrak's Red Cap service, available in many train stations, is invaluable for anyone traveling in a wheelchair.

(https://www.amtrak.com/empire-service-rails-to-recovery)

From a national perspective, the **American Cancer Society** is the primary organization. It provides a multitude of services, including wigs to those who have lost their hair while undergoing chemotherapy.

(http://www.cancer.org/)

Don't be afraid or ashamed to seek help. The organizations were created to support those who need it. Ask social workers and other patients about what they have found most helpful.

# Books and Other References

These are the books I've found most helpful.

## #1 Best Tools and Tips from the Trenches of Breast Cancer

by Mary Olsen Kelly

- **Perfect Paperback:** 192 pages
- **Publisher:** Books Beyond Borders, LLC; 1 edition (September 30, 2006)
- **Language:** English
- **ISBN-10:** 0977894606
- **ISBN-13:** 978-0977894604
- **Publisher Blurb:** Over 100 useful, helpful, comforting and life affirming tools, tips, and stories from the trenches of breast cancer survival. Heartfelt and immediate, this book delivers personal, practical advice from and for breast cancer survivors, family and friends.

Quick, important fact guide.

## 100 Questions & Answers About Cancer Symptoms and Cancer Treatment Side Effects

by Joanne Kelvin, Leslie Tyson

- **Paperback:** 228 pages
- **Publisher:** Jones and Bartlett Publishers, Inc.; 1 edition (September 25, 2004)
- **Language:** English
- **ISBN-10:** 0763726125
- **ISBN-13:** 978-0763726126
- **Publisher Blurb:** Written by cancer professionals and featuring comments from actual patients, this handy guide gives you the information you need to understand the disease and manage treatment side effects.

Great reference guide!

## And in Health: A Guide for Couples Facing Cancer Together
by Dan Shapiro

- **Paperback:** 240 pages
- **Publisher:** Trumpeter; 1 edition (May 14, 2013)
- **Language:** English
- **ISBN-10:** 161180017X
- **ISBN-13:** 978-1611800173
- **Publisher Blurb:** Dan Shapiro draws on his more than twenty-five years of clinical work as a health psychologist who has researched and worked with couples facing cancer, and on his own experiences of being both the patient and the supporter/advocate.

Valuable and comforting; helped us to remain a couple rather than just a patient and caregiver.

## The Art of Healing: Uncovering Your Inner Wisdom and Potential for Self-Healing
by Bernie Siegel, M.D.

- **Paperback:** 256 pages
- **Publisher:** New World Library; 1 edition (September 3, 2013)
- **Language:** English
- **ISBN-10:** 1608681858
- **ISBN-13:** 978-1608681853
- **Publisher Blurb:** Dr. Bernie S. Siegel, a successful surgeon, took a class from Elisabeth Kübler-Ross that focused on crayon drawing for healing, especially with patients facing life-threatening disease. Siegel incorporated into his practice these techniques – many of which were laughed at by others in the medical community.

This guy is fabulous. I use his book regularly.

## Breast Cancer: The Complete Guide
by Yashar Hirshaut, Peter I. Pressman

- **Paperback:** 432 pages
- **Publisher:** Bantam; 5th Revised ed. edition (September 30, 2008)
- **Language:** English
- **ISBN-10:** 0553385917
- **ISBN-13:** 978-0553385915
- **Publisher Blurb:** Written by two renowned authorities who specialize in the treatment of breast cancer, a surgeon and an oncologist, this lucid step-by-step guide has established itself as the indispensable book women need to make informed decisions about the care that is right for them.

  Great reference to help answer many of my questions.

## Cancer: 50 Essential Things to Do
by Greg Anderson

- **Paperback:** 320 pages
- **Publisher:** Plume; 2013 ed. edition (December 24, 2012)
- **Language:** English
- **ISBN-10:** 0452298288
- **ISBN-13:** 978-04522982
- **Publisher Blurb:** This definitive guide empowers cancer patients and their loved ones to move beyond their disease. The author, a cancer survivor, has designed this book for the recently diagnosed, those with recurring symptoms, and those who are well but have a lingering fear that the disease may strike again.

  Quick bullets

## Difficult Conversations
by Celia Engel Bandman

- **Spiral-bound Paperback with DVD:** 35 pages
- **Publisher:** Center for Communications in Medicine, a division of the Institute of Medical Humanism, copyright 2013
- **Language:** English
- **Publisher Blurb:** The workbook uses thematically grouped video segments of real patients' reflections as a framework for guided writing prompts designed to help patients identify and communicate their priorities for treatment and beyond.

Valuable

## Dr. Susan Love's Breast Book
by Susan M. Love & Karen Lindsey (Contributor)

- **Paperback:** 704 pages
- **Publisher:** Da Capo Lifelong Books; Reprint edition (September 8, 2015)
- **Language:** English
- **ISBN-10:** 0738218219
- **ISBN-13:** 978-0738218212
- **Publisher Blurb:** For more than two decades, readers faced with a diagnosis of breast cancer have relied on Dr. Susan Love's Breast Book to guide them through the frightening thicket of research and opinion to find the best options for their particular situations.

Valuable reference guide, very scientific but helped interpret information I got from doctor; like a dictionary.

## The Emerging DreamHealer
by Adam

- **Paperback**: 192 pages
- **Publisher:** Plume (September 29, 2006)
- **Language:** English
- **ISBN-10**: 0452287308
- **ISBN-13**: 978-0452287303
- **Publisher Blurb:** Adam instructs readers on how to tap into their own healing abilities through the use of his dramatic visualization techniques. In the quantum world everything we can imagine is possible – including the improvement of our health and well-being.

> My Reiki practitioner gave it to me. You have to be a believer in healers, which I am. Some are frauds, and some are very gifted. Some of his visualizations of burning the cancer out are remarkable.

## Kicking Cancer in the Kitchen: The Girlfriend's Cookbook and Guide to Using Real Food to Fight Cancer
by Annette Ramke, Kendall Scott

- **Paperback:** 352 pages
- **Publisher:** Running Press Adult; 1 edition (October 2, 2012)
- **Language:** English
- **ISBN-10:** 0762446773
- **ISBN-13:** 978-0762446773
- **Publisher Blurb:** Authors are cancer survivors. Here they share girlfriend-style, real-life knowledge and experience about the healing power of food, along with their stories of cancer ups and downs—with more than 100 recipes for fighting cancer and soothing symptoms of treatment.

> Valuable resource for both of us during treatment and we continue to use today

## Natural Strategies for Cancer Patients
by Russell Blaylock M.D.

- **Paperback:** 304 pages
- **Publisher**: Kensington; 1 edition (October 1, 2003)
- **Language:** English
- **ISBN-10:** 9780758202215
- **ISBN-13:** 978-0758202215
- **Publisher Blurb:** Cancer and current cancer treatments wage war on the body, but Blaylock has developed an easy-to-follow program to fight back naturally.

> Great reference guide to complement our medical treatments

## Prepare for Surgery, Heal Faster with Relaxation and Quick Start CD: A Guide of Mind-Body Techniques
by Peggy Huddleston

- **Paperback:** 267 pages
- **Publisher:** Angel River Press; 5th ed. edition (May 10, 2013)
- **Language:** English
- **ISBN-10:** 0964575728
- **ISBN-13:** 978-0964575721
- **Publisher Blurb:** This book shows you how to use mind-body techniques to reduce anxiety, use 23 to 50 percent less pain medication, and heal faster. Documented by research, it is recommended at leading hospitals across the US.

> I used this as a resource before each surgery. I continue the relaxation and meditation practices.

## Radical Remission: Surviving Cancer Against All Odds
### By Kelly A. Turner

- **Paperback:** 336 pages
- **Publisher:** HarperOne; (September 15, 2015)
- **Language:** English
- **ISBN-10:** 0062268740
- **ISBN-13:** 978-0062268747
- **Publisher Blurb:** Dr. Kelly A. Turner, founder of the Radical Remission Project, uncovers nine factors that can lead to a spontaneous remission from cancer – even after conventional medicine has failed.

> I listened to her speak before I read her book. This validates many of my ideas and pushes me to "walk the walk" even more.

## Spontaneous Healing: How to Discover and Embrace Your Body's Natural Ability to Maintain and Heal Itself
### by Andrew Weil

- **Mass Market Paperback**: 384 pages
- **Publisher:** Ballantine Books (April 4, 2000)
- **Language**: English
- **ISBN-10:** 0804117942
- **ISBN-13**: 978-0804117944
- **Publisher Blurb:** Dr. Andrew Weil shows how spontaneous healing has worked to resolve life-threatening diseases, severe trauma, and chronic pain.

> This is my all-time favorite book and doctor. I use it for everything, not just this journey.

# Lindy's Life

## Nurse – Entrepreneur – Volunteer – Health Advocate – Family Member

## Early Years

Lindy Sanders was born in Bennington, Vermont, in 1956. Her family moved to Milford, Connecticut, where she lived with her mother, step-father, brother and sister, and attended school there.

## Nurse

After trying out several colleges in Connecticut, Lindy joined the Army in 1976, and became a Military Army Nurse. During her ten years in the military and reserves, she traveled extensively, being stationed in Alabama, Texas, California, Georgia, and Colorado.

Lindy married a fellow soldier, John Brooks, in 1978, and credits the military experience with helping her develop many of her strengths: self-discipline, work ethic, and civic responsibility.

She continued nursing after leaving the military, and had two children, Matthew in 1980 and Megan in 1982. By 1984, Lindy was divorced from her first husband and moved to Vermont, where she met and married her second husband and has lived there ever since.

## Entrepreneur

Lindy's first foray into starting her own business was in response to her own needs. She was working with two small children and could not find quality child care. Her solution was to start her own home daycare, then open Country Daycare Center with her mother.

From there she was recruited by the State of Vermont to start an inter-generational daycare center at the Vermont Veterans' Home. Its success was followed by her opening another daycare center, Generations, in Bennington.

Ready for new challenges, Lindy opened an educational supply and toy store called Apple Core in Bennington, and served as an event planner and marketer for Green River Inn in Sandgate, Vermont.

Lindy met Kevin Lynch, owner of Kevin's Sports Bar and Restaurant in North Bennington, in 1998 while pitching him an advertising campaign. Three years later, they married, and Lindy assumed many new responsibilities as co-owner of one of the best restaurants in the Bennington area. They sold the restaurant in 2016.

In 2018, Lindy was hired by Southern Vermont Health Center to manage the Centennial Fair, a celebration of the hospital's 100 years in Bennington. She also served as Program Manager of the Garlic Fest for the tenth year.

## Volunteer

Beginning her commitment to community volunteering as a teenager in Connecticut, Lindy won a scholarship for donating the most hours as a Candy-Striper, at age 15.

Since then she has served in many community service capacities:

- President of Board of Directors for Bennington County Child Care Association
- North Bennington School Board
- President of Bennington Chamber of Commerce
- Events Chairman for Bennington Chamber of Commerce where she led many functions such as:
  - Moose Fest
  - Catamount Fest
  - Garlic Fest
  - Winter Fest
  - Vermont Christmas Tree in Washington, D.C.
- Vermont State Chamber of Commerce
- Bennington Rotary Club / Past President
- Founding Board Member of WBTN public radio station
- Board member at Park McCullough House
- Founding member Northshaft Lions Community skateboard park
- Board Member of John G. McCullough Free Library
- Board member of CAT-TV, Bennington's Public Access Television station.

# Health Advocate

When Lindy's niece was born with an a 104-degree temperature caused by an unknown infection, medical staff called in a priest for last rites. Lindy threw a fit. She demanded that they take the baby to a Neo-Natal unit where the baby could be properly diagnosed. She called everyone she could think of, including the Governor, to get the infant air-lifted by people in Haz-Mat suits to Burlington's Fletcher Allen Hospital (now the University of Vermont Medical Center) where the baby was diagnosed with Group B strep Disease, an infection that can lead to life-threatening complications in newborns. That baby is now twenty-four years old.

That was Lindy's first experience in Health Advocacy. During her recent experiences in the medical world as patient and caregiver, Lindy has continued her role of health advocate for her husband, her friends, her family, and herself.

She has helped start a local group, Bennington Holistic Healing Practitioners (BHHP) to provide the surrounding Bennington-area with easy access to both holistic and natural healing medical providers and professionals. Lindy helped the group create a tremendously successful Wellness Fair in April, 2018.

Lindy is an active member and serves on the board of the Center for Communication in Medicine's Speak Sooner program where she frequently participates in panel discussions with patients and caregivers.

As a member of the Cancer Sucks team of the Cancer Center Community Crusaders, Lindy is helping "give back" to the community that has supported her and Kevin in their journey.

## Family Member

Overarching all other roles are the ones that mean the most to Lindy:

- Daughter
- Sister
- Aunt
- Wife
- Mother
- Mimi and Mema, her grandchildren's names for her
- Friend.

# Lindy's Team

# A Diverse Team

Lindy's travels down the speed-bump-filled cancer journey have been supported by a big, messy team — medical providers, integrative and wholistic health practitioners, support professionals, friends, neighbors, and most importantly, family.

## The Professionals

> Without these wonderful people on my team, I don't think I could have made it this far. They provided their expertise, their strength, and their tissues when I wept. I want them all to know how much I am grateful for them.

### Health Care Providers
- Dr. Iyengar, Breast oncologist, Memorial Sloan
- Dr. Sacchini , Breast surgeon, Memorial Sloan
- Dr. Coit, Melanoma surgeon, Memorial Sloan
- Dr. Marchetti, Dermatologist, Memorial Sloane
- Dr . Salem, Surgeon, SVMC
- Dr. Friscia, Primary Physician
- Bennington Physical Therapy
- SVMC Physical Therapy, Lymphedema therapy
- Mary Bradley, Lymphedema Therapy
- The Pharmacy and staff
- Dr. Baker, Dentist
- Dr. George, Infection control
- Dr. Shoushtari, Melanoma oncologist
- Bayada Home Health team

## Integrative and Holistic Practitioners

- Lisa Verschoor,  Astrologer
- Alicja Bialasiewicz, Angel Therapy Practitioner
- Everley St. Peter, Reiki Master
- Dr. Nancy Burns, Chiropractic Physician
- Bendheim Integrative Medicine Center at Memorial Sloan Kettering
- Stella Connors, Health Coach
- Laurie Jessman, Reflexology
- Leeann Harrington, Massage Therapist
- Cindy Reilly, Acupuncturist
- Bethany Boulger, Lomi Lomi massage
- Dr. Lynn Lind, Biofeedback and homeopathic
- Joyce Getty, Biofeedback
- Betsy Browning, Shen

## Support Professionals: Physical, Emotional and Spiritual

- Penny Rich, pastor
- Deborah J. Lewis, Counseling, Mindfulness-Based Stress Reduction
- Lori Vadakin, Therapist
- Julie Crosier, Personal Trainer
- Dr. Bernie and Celia Bandman, Center for Communication in Medicine

# Friends and Neighbors

I have been blessed with a group of friends and neighbors who have cheered me up, thrown me parties, given me rides to appointments, stayed overnight to give Kevin a break, sent me cards, listened when I wanted to talk, and talked to me when I didn't.

Beth, Mary, and Peg are long-time friends that I met when our children were in nursery school. We raised our children together. We laugh together and cry together. But mostly we have fun together.

Pat Soto has opened doors for Kevin and me at Sloan Kettering. She has helped us navigate their system, has visited us when we were hospitalized, and has regularly been the friendly face in the waiting room when we arrive for another appointment or procedure. I cannot thank her enough.

Our friends and employees from the restaurant have been a steady source of support. They have had fundraisers and fun-raisers when they all dressed in team shirts to wish Kevin luck for his surgery.

I have long-time friends from Rotary, the Chamber, and many strong professional women, all of whom have provided wisdom, prayers, endless support.

## My Family

My family are all saints!

Kevin's large Irish Catholic family have supported me through his illness and through mine. My sisters-in-law have taken their turns as night nurses.

My sister, Sandy, texts me, giving me words of encouragement throughout this long-term battle, and comes to assist with caretaking when I need her.

I have raised two incredible children – my daughter, Megan Lynn, and son, Matthew John, who have provided me their continued support, including nearly dumping me out of wheelchairs, and have made me so proud and grateful.

My five wonderful grandchildren, Lauren, Ava, Chase, Benjamin, and Ryan, are my primary source of joy. Their photos and videos keep me going when I feel like quitting.

My mother, Leone, has been with me through many emergency room visits and many sleepless nights being caring, supportive, and always there.

And Kevin, my wonderful husband, has never faltered. He is my soulmate, caregiver, and personal comedian. And certainly, my personal chef.

I am so very blessed!

# Acknowledgements

I would like to thank the many people who assisted me in writing this book, particularly these:

Jane Radocchia, Catherine McClure, and Suzanne Kirkpatrick for suggesting me as someone to help Lindy with a book

Dawn Rodrigues, Brenda Barnhill, Pam Long, Jane Radocchia, Claudia Dalton, and my writing group – the Scribble Sisters – for encouragement, early readings, advice, and editing.

And of course, Lindy Lynch, whose story I have tried to tell with as much humor, honesty, and heart as she does.

# About the Author

**Kathy Wagenknecht** lives in Bennington, Vermont, in a historic "dual living" house with two border collies and a talented painter.

Visit her at her website: **kathywagenknecht.com**

# Cancer Center Community Crusaders

The Cancer Center Community Crusaders (The 4Cs) provide financial, physical, and emotional support to members of the community and their families as they strive to obtain the best cancer care and treatment possible. All funds raised by the Cancer Center Community Crusaders stay in the communities of Bennington and Windham counties in Vermont and nearby New York and Massachusetts. Patients need not receive treatment at Southwestern Vermont Regional Cancer Center to be eligible for funds.

All proceeds from this book will be donated to The 4Cs.

18894108R00057

Made in the USA
Middletown, DE
09 December 2018